I

♥

Dad

I ♥ Dad

200 Great Quotes & Reasons Why

Fathers Are Awesome

Arranged by

JACKIE CORLEY

Hatherleigh Press is committed to preserving
and protecting the natural resources of the earth.
Environmentally responsible and sustainable practices
are embraced within the company's mission statement.

Visit us at www.hatherleighpress.com.

I ♥ Dad

Library of Congress Cataloging-in-Publication Data

is available.

ISBN: 978-1-57826-942-6

Printed in the United States

10 9 8 7 6 5 4 3 2 1

For my father, Jack Corley:
Thank you for always being the person
I could turn to and for lifting me up
whenever I stumbled. I love you.

Contents

Introduction

A FATHER IS A FIRST AND FOREMOST A protector. In a world so often overwhelming and scary, a father is there to hold a child's hand to cross a busy street; to vanquish the monsters in the closet; to pick us up when we fall off our bike. And that protective instinct lasts a lifetime—dads are the first person we think to call when the water heater blows; when we're unsure whether to take a job offer; or when we break down on the side of the road. In those moments when we are most unsure about where our life is taking us, we know that we can count on our dad to guide us.

The lessons learned from a father become etched into our memory. No matter the circumstance, we don't have to ask, "What would dad do?" We already know the answer. It may have been by his words or by his quiet example, but it is through our dads that we learn how to navigate life.

A father can also be counted on to be our most vocal cheerleader and our most honest critic. When we are unsure whether we are ready to step up onto a stage or take a giant leap off the diving board, it is dad's confident assurance that gives us confidence in ourselves.

The secret behind all of these great gifts—how fathers are our biggest supporters, our fiercest protectors, and our greatest teachers—is that the act of raising children brings out the best in them. This collection is a testament, a celebration of the role fathers play in our lives and the way fatherhood helps men realize their fullest potential.

A Child's Protector

A father is the strongest person in the world and a superhero in the eyes of his young child. Fathers offer protection from an uncertain world, a place of strength and safety where we can grow into ourselves without worry.

Dads don't need to be tall and broad-shouldered and clever. Love makes them so.

—PAM BROWN

• • •

He adopted a role called being a father so that his child would have something mythical and infinitely important: a protector.

—TOM WOLFE

• • •

A great dad is always there, but parks down the street so your friends don't see you get dropped off.

—TINA NEIDLEIN

I think a father is someone,
Who loves unconditionally,
There is no perfect formula,
To who a father can be.

—JULIE HÉBERT

• • •

A father's duty is to make his home a place of happiness and joy.

—EZRA TAFT BENSON

• • •

A father's love is forever imprinted on his child's heart.

—JENNIFER WILLIAMSON

What I love most about fatherhood is the opportunity to be a part of the development process of a new life.

—SEAL

• • •

Every father bears a fundamental obligation to do right by their children.

—BARACK OBAMA

• • •

Great fathers don't find fault. Great fathers find solutions.

—REED MARKHAM

It is easier to build strong children than to repair broken men.

—FREDERICK DOUGLASS

•   •   •

Where parents do too much for their children, the children will not do much for themselves.

—ELBERT HUBBARD

•   •   •

We cannot protect our children from life. Therefore, it is essential that we prepare them for it.

—RUDOLF DREIKURS

Your children need your presence more than your presents.

—JESSE JACKSON

• • •

Parents are the bones on which children cut their teeth.

—PETER USTINOV

• • •

You are the bows from which your children as living arrows are sent forth.

—KHALIL GIBRAN

My father didn't do anything unusual. He only did what dads are supposed to do—be there.

—MAX LUCADO

• • •

By profession I am a soldier and take great pride in that fact, but I am prouder, infinitely prouder, to be a father. A soldier destroys in order to build; the father only builds, never destroys. The one has the potentialities of death; the other embodies creation and life.

—GENERAL DOUGLAS MACARTHUR

The strongest, toughest men all have compassion. They're not heartless and cold. You have to be man enough to have compassion—to care about people and about your children.

—DENZEL WASHINGTON

• • •

All we have of freedom—all we use or know
This our fathers bought for us, long and
    long ago.

—RUDYARD KIPLING

What I've realized is that life doesn't count for much unless you're willing to do your small part to leave our children—all of our children—a better world. Even if it's difficult... That is our ultimate responsibility as fathers and parents. We try. We hope.

—BARACK OBAMA

• • •

The father who laughs with his kids more than he lectures them is way ahead of the game.

—HARRY STEIN

Children desperately need to know—and to hear in ways they understand and remember—that they're loved and valued by mom and dad.

—GARY SMALLEY

• • •

If we never have headaches through rebuking our children, we shall have plenty of heartaches when they grow up.

—CHARLES SPURGEON

Fatherhood is a relationship of love and under-standing. It is power and action. It is counsel and instruction.

—DR. MYLES MUNROE

• • •

My dad never pushed me but the big thing is that he helped me by going out in the backyard and playing with me.

—BART STARR

Affirming words from moms and dads are like light switches. Speak a word of affirmation at the right moment in a child's life and it's like lighting up a whole roomful of possibilities.

—GARY SMALLEY

• • •

Dad's love waits up when the rest of the world has already turned out the lights.

—DIANA MANNING

Being a father means you have to think fast on your feet. You must be judicious, wise, brave, tender, and willing to put on a frilly hat and sit down to a pretend tea party.

—MATTHEW BUCKLEY

• • •

One father is enough to govern one hundred sons, but not a hundred sons one father.

—GEORGE HERBERT

It's your dad who tells you that you are
beautiful.
It's your dad who picks you up over his head
and carries you on his shoulders.
It's your dad who will fight the monsters under
your bed.
It's your dad who tells you that you are worth a
lot, so don't settle for the first guy who tells
you you're pretty.

—SHEILA WALSH

• • •

No matter how old we are, we still need our dads,
and wonder how we'll get by without them.

—JENNIFER WILLIAMSON

We may not be able to prepare the future for our children, but we can at least prepare our children for the future.

—FRANKLIN D. ROOSEVELT

• • •

Fatherhood is not a matter of station or wealth; it is a matter of desire, diligence, and determination to see one's family exalted in the celestial kingdom. If that prize is lost, nothing else really matters.

—EZRA TAFT BENSON

Fatherhood:
A Man's Most
Important Role

The only measure of success for someone who has reared a child is their success as a parent. For any man who has raised a child, fatherhood is the most important responsibility they'll have.

Father is the noblest title a man can be given. It is more than a biological role. It signifies a patriarch, a leader, an exemplar, a confidant, a teacher, a hero, a friend.

—ROBERT L. BACKMAN

• • •

Fatherhood is not an easy assignment, but it ranks among the most imperative ever given, in time or eternity.

—JEFFREY R. HOLLAND

Not every successful man is a good father. But every good father is a successful man.

—ROBERT DUVALL

• • •

Being a father makes everything in the world make sense.

—CAMERON MATHISON

• • •

I'm a father; that's what matters most. Nothing matters more.

—GORDON BROWN

Blessed indeed is the man who hears many gentle voices call him father.

—LYDIA M. CHILD

• • •

Being a dad is my most important job because it not only affects my children, but their children and many generations to come.

—MARK DOMINIK

• • •

The toughest job in the world isn't being a president. It's being a parent.

—BILL CLINTON

One of the greatest titles in the world is parent, and one of the biggest blessings in the world is to have parents to call mom and dad.

—JIM DEMINT

• • •

I take pride in knowing that of all the things I have accomplished, no success or honor is greater than that of being a father.

—LES BROWN

I didn't think it was going to be this fun. But everything just gets heightened when you have a baby. The volume gets turned up on life. I never knew I could be this happy, and that's the truth.

—JIMMY FALLON

• • •

Fathers, like mothers, are not born. Men grow into fathers and fathering is a very important stage in their development.

—DAVID GOTTESMAN

The nature of impending fatherhood is that you are doing something that you are unqualified to do, and then you become qualified while doing it.

—JOHN GREEN

• • •

[Fatherhood is] the greatest thing that could ever happen. You can't explain it until it happens; it's like telling somebody what water feels like before they've ever swam in it.

—MICHAEL BUBLÉ

When you have kids, you see life through different eyes. You feel love more deeply and are maybe a little more compassionate.

—DAVE GROHL

• • •

No duty in my life is more important or more sacred than my role as a husband and father. That is where my true character is most accurately seen, and it is the best single gauge of my overall success or failure as a leader and role model.

—JOHN MACARTHUR

Being a father has been, without a doubt, my greatest source of achievement, pride, and inspiration. Fatherhood has taught me about unconditional love, reinforced the importance of giving back and taught me how to be a better person.

—NAVEEN JAIN

• • •

Being a father is the most important role I will ever play and if I don't do this well, no other thing I do really matters.

—MICHAEL JOSEPHSON

Once you've launched into parenthood, you'll need all your best skills, self-control, good judgment and patience. But at the same time there is nothing like the thrill and exhilaration that come from watching that bright, cheerful, inquisitive, creative, eccentric and even goofy child you have raised flourish and shine. That's what keeps you going, and what, in the end, makes it all worthwhile.

—LAWRENCE BALTER

• • •

Life affords no greater responsibility, no greater privilege, than the raising of the next generation.

—C. EVERETT KOOP

By profession, I am a soldier and take great pride in that fact. But I am also prouder, infinitely prouder, to be a father. A soldier destroys in order to build; the father only builds, never destroys.

—GENERAL DOUGLAS MACARTHUR

• • •

In my career, there's many things I've won and many things I've achieved, but for me, my greatest achievement is my children and my family.

—DAVID BECKHAM

Being a father, being a friend, those are the things that make me feel successful.

—WILLIAM HURT

• • •

Becoming a father is one of the most important, exciting, absorbing and life-changing events in a man's life. There is nothing like it, and nothing that can fully prepare you for it.

—TIM ATKINSON

Any fool can have a child. That doesn't make you a father. It's the courage to raise a child that makes you a father.

—BARACK OBAMA

• • •

Never is a man more of a man than when he is the father of a newborn.

—MATTHEW MCCONAUGHEY

Until you have a son of your own you will never know the joy, the love beyond feeling that resonates in the heart of a father as he looks upon his son. You will never know the sense of honor that makes a man want to be more than he is and to pass something good and hopeful into the hands of his son. And you will never know the heartbreak of the fathers who are haunted by the personal demons that keep them from being the men they want their sons to be.

—KENT NERBURN

• • •

A father is a man who expects his son to be as good a man as he meant to be.

—FRANK A. CLARK

Fatherhood must be more than a matter of DNA. A man must choose to be a father in the same way that a woman chooses to be a mother.

—MEL FEIT

• • •

The most important thing a father can do for his children is to love their mother.

—REVEREND THEODORE HESBURGH

• • •

Being a father is sometimes my hardest but always my most rewarding job.

—BARACK OBAMA

To be a father requires patience, love and giving up the 'all about me' attitude.

—CATHERINE PULSIFER

• • •

Fatherhood is a lifetime responsibility with its challenges, sweetness and bitterness.

—OLUWAKEMI OLA-OJO

• • •

The end product of child raising is not the child but the parent.

—FRANK PITTMAN

The heart of a father is the masterpiece of nature.

—ANTOINE-FRANÇOIS PRÉVOST

• • •

Leading a family is the hardest job a man can ever have.

—DAVE RAMSEY

• • •

Becoming a dad means you have to be a role model for your son and be someone he can look up to.

—WAYNE ROONEY

What it's like to be a parent: It's one of the hardest things you'll ever do but in exchange it teaches you the meaning of unconditional love.

—NICHOLAS SPARKS

• • •

The guys who fear becoming fathers don't understand that fathering is not something perfect men do, but something that perfects the man.

—FRANK PITTMAN

Fatherhood has made me more vulnerable than any other experience. It has humbled me, healed me and transformed me.

—CRAIG WILKINSON

• • •

Every dad, if he takes time out of his busy life to reflect upon his fatherhood, can learn ways to become an even better dad.

— JACK BAKER

My dad never pushed me but the big thing is that he helped me by going out in the backyard and playing with me.

—BART STARR

• • •

A father is always making his baby into a little woman. And when she is a woman he turns her back again.

—ENID BAGNOLD

I've jumped out of helicopters and done some daring stunts and played baseball in a professional stadium, but none of it means anything compared to being somebody's daddy.

—CHRIS PRATT

• • •

A man's worth is measured by how he parents his children. What he gives them, what he keeps away from them, the lessons he teaches and the lessons he allows them to learn on their own.

—LISA ROGERS

There's something like a line of gold thread running through a man's words when he talks to his daughter, and gradually over the years it gets to be long enough for you to pick up in your hands and weave into a cloth that feels like love itself.

—JOHN GREGORY BROWN

• • •

Certain is it that there is no kind of affection so purely angelic as of a father to a daughter. In love to our wives there is desire; to our sons, ambition, but to our daughters there is something which there are no words to express.

—JOSEPH ADDISON

A truly great man never puts away the simplicity of a child.

—CONFUCIUS

• • •

A girl's father is the first man in her life, and probably the most influential.

—DAVID JEREMIAH

• • •

Being a daddy's girl is like having permanent armor for the rest of your life.

—ANONYMOUS

The father of a daughter is nothing but a high-class hostage. A father turns a stony face to his sons, berates them, shakes his antlers, paws the ground, snorts, runs them off into the underbrush, but when his daughter puts her arm over his shoulder and says, "Daddy, I need to ask you something," he is a pat of butter in a hot frying pan.

—GARRISON KEILLOR

• • •

His heritage to his children wasn't words or possessions, but an unspoken treasure, the treasure of his example as a man and a father.

—WILL ROGERS, JR.

A real man loves his wife, and places his family as the most important thing in life. Nothing has brought me more peace and content in life than simply being a good husband and father.

—FRANK ABAGNALE

Our Biggest Supporter

Fathers can be counted on to be a child's biggest fan and to provide foundational support. By being present and positive, fathers provide a sense of stability and security, allowing children to feel seen, heard, and loved—all of which has a profound impact on our sense of self-confidence and self-worth.

My dad encouraged us to fail. Growing up, he would ask us what we failed at that week. If we didn't have something, he would be disappointed. It changed my mind set at an early age that failure is not the outcome, failure is not trying. Don't be afraid to fail.

—SARA BLAKELY

• • •

It is not flesh and blood, but heart which makes us fathers and sons.

—FRIEDRICH SCHILLER

There will always be a few people who have the courage to love what is untamed inside us. One of those men is my father.

—ALISON LOHMAN

• • •

If a child is to keep alive his inborn sense of wonder, he needs the companionship of at least one adult who can share it, rediscovering with him the joy, excitement, and mystery of the world we live in.

—RACHEL CARSON

It was my father who taught me to value myself.

—DAWN FRENCH

• • •

Fatherly love is the act of giving your life for the sake of someone else's needs.

—NATE DALLAS

• • •

A child needs encouragement like a plant needs water.

—RUDOLF DREIKURS

My dad says he likes to bask in my glow.

—ROBERT PATTINSON

• • •

Fathers provide not only support but also encouragement.

—DR. JAMES DOBSON

• • •

Show as much interest in what your children tell you as they have in telling you.

—WES FESLER

A child seldom needs a good talking to as a good listening to.

—ROBERT BREAULT

• • •

A father is the one friend upon whom we can always rely. In the hour of need, when all else fails, we remember him upon whose knees we sat when children, and who soothed our sorrows; and even though he may be unable to assist us, his mere presence serves to comfort and strengthen us.

—ÉMILE GABORIAU

When you need real understanding, when you need someone to care, when you need someone to guide you... A father's always there.

—THOMAS J. LANGLEY

• • •

Be kind to thy father, for when thou were young, who loved thee so fondly as he? He caught the first accents that fell from thy tongue, and joined in thy innocent glee.

—MARGARET ANN COURTNEY

More broadly across time and cultures, it seems, one perennial piece of advice to father has been the importance of acting tenderly toward their children. The New Father, it turns out, is an old story.

—DAVID BLANKENHORN

• • •

The quality of a father can be seen in the goals, dreams and aspirations he sets not only for himself, but for his family.

—REED MARKHAM

My father used to say that it's never too late to do anything you wanted to do. And he said, 'You never know what you can accomplish until you try.'

—MICHAEL JORDAN

• • •

If you raise your children to feel that they can accomplish any goal or task they decide upon, you will have succeeded as a parent and you will have given your children the greatest of all blessings.

—BRIAN TRACY

The father who would taste the essence of his fatherhood must turn back from the plane of his experience, take with him the fruits of his journey and begin again beside his child, marching step by step over the same old road.

—ANGELO PATRI

• • •

I have always had the feeling I could do anything and my dad told me I could. I was in college before I found out he might be wrong.

—ANN RICHARDS

When my father didn't have my hand, he had my back.

—LINDA POINDEXTER

• • •

You do not have to make your children into wonderful people. You just have to remind them that they are wonderful people. If you do this consistently from the day they are born they will believe it easily.

—WILLIAM MARTIN

I love my dad. He's the biggest thing in my life. He taught me and he straightened me out and he kept me in line. If it hadn't been for him standing behind me and pushing me and driving me, I wouldn't be where I am today.

—ANTHONY PERKINS

• • •

Dad gave me two pieces of advice. One was, 'No matter how good you think you are, there are people better than you.' But he was an optimist too; his other advice: 'Never worry about rejection. Every day is a new beginning.'

—JOHN RITTER

Love is at the root of all healthy discipline. The desire to be loved is a powerful motivation for children to behave in ways that give their parents pleasure rather than displeasure. it may even be our own long-ago fear of losing our parents' love that now sometimes makes us uneasy about setting and maintaining limits. We're afraid we'll lose the love of our children when we don't let them have their way.

—FRED ROGERS

• • •

Good parents give their children roots and wings. Roots to know where home is, wings to fly away and exercise what's been taught them.

—JONAS SALK

My father gave me the greatest gift anyone could give another person, he believed in me.

—JIM VALVANO

• • •

Children will not remember you for the material things you gave them but for the feeling that you cherished them.

—RICHARD L. EVANS

• • •

My mother gave me my drive, but my father gave me my dreams. Thanks to him, I could see a future.

—LIZA MINNELLI

There are only two lasting bequests we can hope to give our children. One of these is roots, the other, wings.

—JOHANN WOLFGANG VON GOETHE

• • •

I am 30 years old, and I still find great power in my own dad telling me it's possible. I still find great power in my own dad telling me I can do it.

—DANIEL PEARCE

What's a good investment? Go home from work early and spend the afternoon throwing a ball around with your son.

—BEN STEIN

• • •

The greatest gifts you can give your children are the roots of responsibility and the wings of independence.

—DENIS WAITLEY

My dad believed in me, even when I didn't. He always knew I could do this. I'm sure that everyone in Reading remembers how much he talked about me. I thought that was sweet, but really I just wasn't as sure it would happen. So, I just love my dad for believing in his little girl.

—TAYLOR SWIFT

Teaching by Example

A father is one of the first teachers a child has. He leads by quiet example and his actions provide an education that lasts a lifetime. As children, we learn by observing and imitating our father's actions, attitudes, and values—lessons which form the bedrock of the people we grow up to be.

My father didn't tell me how to live; he lived, and let me watch him do it.

—CLARENCE BUDINGTON KELLAND

• • •

Children are educated by what the grown-up is and not by his talk.

—CARL JUNG

• • •

What we are teaches the child far more than what we say, so we must be what we want our children to become.

—JOSEPH CHILTON PEARCE

My father was my teacher. But most importantly he was a great dad.

—BEAU BRIDGES

• • •

Children have never been very good at listening to their elders, but they have never failed to imitate them.

—JAMES A. BALDWIN

• • •

What I learned most from my father wasn't anything he said; it was just the way he behaved.

—JEFF BRIDGES

I love my father as the stars—he's a bright shining example and a happy twinkling in my heart.

—TERRI GUILLEMETS

• • •

I watched a small man with thick calluses on both hands work 15 and 16 hours a day. I saw him once literally bleed from the bottoms of his feet, a man who came here uneducated, alone, unable to speak the language, who taught me all I needed to know about faith and hard work by the simple eloquence of his example.

—MARIO CUOMO

Children learn more from what you are than what you teach.

—W. E. B. DU BOIS

• • •

Life doesn't come with an instruction book; that's why we have fathers.

—H. JACKSON BROWN, JR.

• • •

Don't worry that children never listen to you; worry that they are always watching you.

—ROBERT FULGHUM

The attitude you have as a parent is what your kids will learn from more than what you tell them. They don't remember what you try to teach them. They remember what you are.

—JIM HENSON

• • •

I believe that what we become depends on what our fathers teach us at odd moments, when they aren't trying to teach us. We are formed by the little scraps of wisdom.

—UMBERTO ECO

A good father. A man with a head, a heart, and a soul. A man capable of listening, of leading and respecting a child, and not of drowning his own defects in him. Someone whom a child will not only love because he's his father, but will also admire for the person he is. Someone he would want to grow up to resemble.

—CARLOS RUIZ ZAFÓN

• • •

The most important thing that parents can teach their children is how to get along without them.

—FRANK A. CLARK

Every son quotes his father, in words and in deeds.

—TERRI GUILLEMETS

• • •

Every father should remember that one day his son will follow his example rather than his advice.

—CHARLES F. KETTERING

• • •

Your children will become what you are; so be what you want them to be.

—DAVID BLY

Good fathers not only tell us how to live, they show us.

—MARK TWAIN

• • •

I talk and talk and talk, and I haven't taught people in 50 years what my father taught by example in one week.

—MARIO CUOMO

• • •

Every day, you are teaching your children what it means to be a father.

—LARRY M. GIBSON

Lecturing to you will not make you a better father, because fatherhood is not a matter of conscious information; it's a matter of having the right frame of mind and the right pattern of reactions to children's behaviors and needs.

—ROB WAGNER

• • •

He that will have his son have respect for him and his orders, must himself have a great reverence for his son.

—JOHN LOCKE

My dad, like any coach, has always stressed the fundamentals. He taught me responsibility, accountability, and the importance of hard work.

—STEVE YOUNG

• • •

Children need models rather than critics.

—JOSEPH JOUBERT

• • •

To bring up a child in the way he should go, travel that way yourself once in a while.

—JOSH BILLINGS

Words have an awesome impact. The impression made by a father's voice can set in motion an entire trend of life.

—GORDON MACDONALD

• • •

The best way to give advice to your children is to find out what they want and then advise them to do it.

—HARRY S. TRUMAN

• • •

You will find that if you really try to be a father, your child will meet you halfway.

—ROBERT BREAULT

It's not only children who grow. Parents do too. As much as we watch to see what our children do with their lives, they are watching us to see what we do with ours. I can't tell my children to reach for the sun. All I can do is reach for it, myself.

—JOYCE MAYNARD

• • •

The words that a father speaks to his children in the privacy of home are not heard by the world, but, as in whispering galleries, they are clearly heard at the end, and by posterity.

—JEAN PAUL RICHTER

When a father gives to his son, both laugh; when a son gives to his father, both cry.

—WILLIAM SHAKESPEARE

• • •

My father taught me how to be a man—and not by instilling in me a sense of machismo or an agenda of dominance. He taught me that a real man doesn't take, he gives; he doesn't use force, he uses logic; doesn't play the role of trouble-maker, but rather, trouble-shooter.

—KEVIN SMITH

Father taught us that opportunity and responsibility go hand in hand. I think we all act on that principle; on the basic human impulse that makes a man want to make the best of what's in him and what's been given him.

—LAURENCE ROCKEFELLER

• • •

My dad has always taught me these words: care and share.

—TIGER WOODS

The father who does not teach his son his duties
is equally guilty with the son who neglects them.

—CONFUCIUS

• • •

When you teach your son, you teach your
son's son.

—THE TALMUD

• • •

An almost perfect relationship with his father
was the earthly root of all his wisdom.

—C.S. LEWIS

A good father believes that he does wisely to encourage enterprise, productive skill, prudent self-denial, and judicious expenditure on the part of his son.

—WILLIAM GRAHAM SUMNER

• • •

My father taught me that the only way you can make good at anything is to practice, and then practice some more.

—PETE ROSE

To be as good as our fathers we must be better, imitation is not discipleship.

—WENDELL PHILLIPS

• • •

One father is more than a hundred schoolmasters.

—GEORGE HERBERT

• • •

A son is not the judge of his father, but the conscience of the father is in his son.

—SIMON SOLOVEYCHIK

I think that my strong determination for justice come from the dynamic personality of my father. I have rarely met a person more fearless and courageous than my father. He is a man of real integrity, deeply committed to moral and ethical principles. If I had a problem, I could always call Daddy.

—MARTIN LUTHER KING, JR.

Unsung Heroes

Only as a child grows older do they truly appreciate all their father has done for them. Fathers quietly go about raising, educating and protecting a child without asking for anything in return. Fathers are unsung heroes in the lives of their children—but that doesn't mean we can't stop and thank them for all they do.

The depth of the love of parents for their children cannot be measured. It is like no other relationship. It exceeds concern for life itself. The love of a parent for a child is continuous, and transcends heartbreak and disappointment.

—JAMES E. FAUST

• • •

He has always provided me a safe place to land and a hard place from which to launch.

—CHELSEA CLINTON

• • •

Dad: a son's first hero, a daughter's first love.

—JOHN WALTER BRATTON

A good father is one of the most unsung, unpraised, unnoticed, and yet one of the most valuable assets in our society.

—BILLY GRAHAM

• • •

It doesn't matter who my father was; it matters who I remember he was.

—ANNE SEXTON

• • •

Dads are most ordinary men turned by love into heroes, adventurers, story-tellers, and singers of song.

—PAM BROWN

I cannot think of any need in childhood as strong as the need for a father's protection.

—SIGMUND FREUD

• • •

To a young boy, a father is a giant from whose shoulders you can see forever.

—PERRY GARFINKEL

• • •

Safe, for a child, is his father's hand, holding him tight.

—MARION C. GARRETTY

The greatest mark of a father is how he treats his children when no one is looking.

—DANIEL PEARCE

• • •

The greatest tribute a boy can give to his father is to say, 'When I grow up, I want to be just like my dad.'

—BILLY GRAHAM

• • •

No man I ever met was my father's equal, and I never loved any other man as much.

—HEDY LAMARR

Fathers are an integral part of the family for their contribution to the household by caregiving and ensuring the healthy development and well-being of children and families.

—OLA AKINMADE

• • •

This is how you can tell a father. He is a man who will play with you even though he has friends his own age to play with.

—JIM LANGDON

It is much easier to become a father than to be one.

—KENT NERBURN

• • •

When all else fails—call Dad!

—SUZANNE BERRY

• • •

Any man can be a father. It takes someone special to be a dad.

—ANNE GEDDES

Average fathers have patience. Good fathers have more patience. Great fathers have an ocean of patience.

—REED MARKHAM

• • •

Confident men have patient fathers.

—ROSE O'KELLY

• • •

Sometimes the poorest man leaves his children the richest inheritance.

—RUTH E. RENKEL

Anyone who does anything to help a child in his life is a hero.

—FRED ROGERS

• • •

Lately all my friends are worried they're turning into their fathers. I'm worried I'm not.

—DAN ZEVIN

• • •

The older I get, the smarter my father seems to get.

—TIM RUSSERT

There's a special place in heaven for caregivers.

—MAUREEN REAGAN

• • •

That's what a father does. Eases the burdens of those he loves. Saves the ones he loves from painful last images that might endure for a lifetime.

—GEORGE SAUNDERS

• • •

My daddy, he was somewhere between God and John Wayne.

—HANK WILLIAMS, JR.

You don't remember the times your dad held your handlebars. You remember the day he let go.

—LENORE SKENAZY

• • •

That is the thankless position of the father in the family-the provider for all, and the enemy of all.

—AUGUST STRINDBERG

• • •

The greatest gift I ever had
Came from God; I call him Dad!

—JOHN WALTER BRATTON

When I was a boy of 14, my father was so ignorant I could hardly stand to have the old man around. But when I got to be 21, I was astonished at how much the old man had learned in seven years.

—MARK TWAIN

• • •

You don't raise heroes, you raise sons. And if you treat them like sons, they'll turn out to be heroes, even if it's just in your own eyes.

—WALTER M. SCHIRRA, SR.

By the time a man realizes that maybe his father was right, he usually has a son who thinks he's wrong.

—CHARLES WADSWORTH

•   •   •

Father! To God himself we cannot give a holier name.

—WILLIAM WORDSWORTH

•   •   •

It is easier for a father to have children than for children to have a real father.

—POPE JOHN XXIII

If there is any immortality to be had among us human beings, it is certainly only in the love that we leave behind. Fathers like mine don't ever die.

—LEO BUSCAGLIA

• • •

Dads are like chocolate chip cookies; they may have chips or be totally nutty, but they are sweet and make the world a better place.

—HILLARY LYTLE

• • •

I decided in my life that I would do nothing that did not reflect positively on my father's life.

—SIDNEY POITIER

It's only when you grow up and step back from him—or leave him for your own home—it's only then that you can measure his greatness and fully appreciate it.

—MARGARET TRUMAN

Conclusion

A FATHER IS ONE OF THE MOST POWER-
ful sources of influences in their child's life.
He's a teacher and a hero, a firm guide and a
friend. Whenever dad opens his mouth, we lean
in close to listen (even when we're at an age where
we pretend not to hear).

The wisdom and love that a father gives his
child lasts a lifetime. Even those who have lost
a father can feel his presence enveloping them
in warmth and security. The knowledge that dad
has always been there to protect us gives us the
strength to bear life's challenges.

Nor is fatherhood a gift only to the child—
becoming a dad helps a man realize his full
potential. Raising a child is a profound gift

and responsibility, one which every good father embraces with a full heart.

From providing emotional support and guidance to modeling positive values and behaviors, fathers play a vital role in shaping who we become. Their influence extends providing food, clothing and shelter—they instill in us a lasting bond that shapes our sense of self-worth, confidence, and identity. As we have seen in the quotations in this collection, fathers make a difference in our lives every single day—in ways both big and small. Let us cherish and honor these unsung heroes by acknowledging the profound impact they have on our lives, and the people we grow to be.